PRAISE FOR *Financial Infidelity*

In *Financial Infidelity,* Laura Whittemore tells a heart-wrenching story of financial betrayal. She offers a clear warning of the devastating consequences of ignoring financial red flags in our most intimate relationships.

> — **Dr. Brad Klontz**, Financial Psychologist, author of *Money Mammoth: Harness the Power of Financial Psychology to Evolve Your Money Mindset, Avoid Extinction, and Crush Your Financial Goal*

Laura Whittemore has written a highly informative book that serves as a real-life series of cautionary tales that every woman should read. Financial Infidelity is a true phenomenon that women are very vulnerable to experiencing. As a Money Coach, I highly recommend reading this book before mixing money in a relationship … it's a gem!

> — **Deborah Price**, author of *The Heart of Money: A Couple's Guide to Creating True Financial Intimacy*, Founder & CEO of The Money Coaching Institute

Financial Infidelity: Love and Theft in Retirement is uniquely written and draws the reader in. This true story will help women recognize the warning signs of a partner who speaks love but acts with deceit. A great read for anyone questioning the love and money in their life.

> — **Barbara Huson,** author of *Rewire for Wealth* and *Overcoming Underearning*

There are illusions associated with love and fear. Laura Whittemore's book is a cautionary tale that should be required reading for all online dating services and relationship therapists.

> — **Ricardo Esparza**, PhD psychologist, Boulder, CO

Financial Infidelity

Love and Theft in Retirement

Conversations with a Victim

LAURA L. WHITTEMORE

CLEAR FOCUS PRESS

Financial Infidelity: Love and Theft in Retirement
Conversations with a Victim
by Laura L. Whittemore

Published by
CLEAR FOCUS PRESS
PO Box 10578
Kalispell, MT 59901
Email: ClearFocusPress@gmail.com

Author email: LauraWhittemoreAuthor@gmail.com

Book Design: Nick Zelinger, NZGraphics.com

ISBN: 978-0-9824094-5-9 (Paper)
ISBN: 978-0-9824094-6-6 (eBook)

LCCN: 2020925632

First Edition

Printed in the United States of America

CONTENTS

PREFACE

This is the true story of my friend who became the victim of financial infidelity and was led down the path of deceit and betrayal by her loving, second husband. When she almost lost all of her retirement funds, she finally confided in me. Our phone conversations over five years eventually revealed the true story, which is written here entirely in dialogue. My friend allowed me to interview her to confirm facts and details which helped to recreate her dialogue and reveal the characters involved.

It is our intention that her story might be a wakeup call for women contemplating marriage in later years. Hopefully, this true story will encourage them to take off the blinders of love and question any red flags that accompany gut reactions. We agreed that her real name and location did not appear in this personal narrative.

PART I
The Setup

PROLOGUE

"Hello?"

"Hello, is this Brenda Chadberg?"

"Yes."

"I'm calling from ABC Debt Consolation and
we have been informed that your VISA credit card
from Chase Bank has over $500 in late fees
with a balance due of $10,750."

*"I don't know what you're talking about because I don't
even have a VISA with Chase Bank."*

"It says here that it was opened September 13, 2015 with
your name as the primary holder."

*"Honestly, I don't understand what you're telling me.
I don't remember receiving any statements to prove
what you're saying. I'm beginning to think this is a scam
call and I'm going to hang up."*

"Before you do that, let me say that it's understandable for you to be surprised because it's possible that someone else in your household may have used your card, that's why you never saw the statements. If that person knows the login information, every transaction can be made online, even receiving the statements to another email address."

"That's impossible and I'm going to hang up now."

"If you decide that you need us in the future, you can reach us at 800-000-0000."

"OK, goodbye."

—————— *September 2015* ——————

"Hello, Brenda."

"Hey, Laura, is this a good time to talk?"

"Perfect! I'm so glad you called because I've been thinking about you and wondering how married life is treating you?"

"Awesome! Steve and I have so much fun together. We just got back from one of his consulting interviews in California, and we stayed at this charming hotel. We ate at the best restaurants and he made sure I scheduled a massage while he was in a business meeting."

"Wow, Steve sure knows how to make you happy!"

"That he does!"

"I saw those gorgeous photos you posted on Facebook of your June wedding in Hawaii. What a stunning setting."

"Did you know Steve planned the entire event to be a simple, private wedding on the beach?"

"No, but I'm not surprised."

"He located this mom and pop business that made the arrangements for the minister, flowers, music and even the photographer. Sounds like an all-in-the family affair, doesn't it?"

Now that's a deal. But how did you feel about not having your friends or family there?"

"Well, he wanted to make our wedding very special, and he has fond memories of that beach. We thought it would be easier for everyone to celebrate at a wedding reception back home."

"Oh, I get it. That does make sense. Anyway, you looked radiant at the reception in August with both of you dressed in wedding white. I'm glad I could be there. I like the way Steve wears a tam backwards. Very European."

"Yeah, I do too. I think the tam adds a little class."

"I also enjoyed meeting Steve's son and daughter and seeing how much your grandchildren have grown. What a catch you are, blond, blue eyed and still petite at sixty-four. You even look younger since you met Steve."

"Thank you! Yes, he continues to plan interesting things for us to do, even on the spur of the moment. Really, life is going quite well… except something unfortunate happened to Steve. That's why I'm calling because I need to talk to you."

"Oh no! Was he in an accident?"

"No, no, nothing like that. Steve's okay, but I have to explain what happened to his retirement fund. This is very confidential and, of course, I trust you."

"Geez, Brenda! This must be serious! You know I'm here for you. So, what's happening?"

"Actually, I learned about this when we were on our honeymoon in Hawaii. Steve told me not to tell anyone. He received a call from his friend and when he hung up, he had this shocked look on his face. He explained that a year ago, he transferred his retirement funds to an investment company that his fraternity brother

recommended and worked at for several years. It seems there was an internal fraud, and unfortunately, Steve and many of his friends lost money."

"Oh my god, Brenda! That must have devastated him! How much did he have invested?"

"He lost about $700,000!"

"For real? That's a lot of money! Is that like all his savings?"

"Nearly! Anyway, he seemed positive it would eventually be resolved, so I didn't worry about it. But earlier this month, he told me he needed $30,000 to pay his attorney to investigate the fraud. Steve mentioned that the investment company was in Houston. He stressed that I shouldn't tell anyone because his attorney didn't want anything to disrupt the investigation."

"Brenda, doesn't he have a savings account or other resources?"

"He finished a long-term consulting job about a month ago, and that's why we took the trip to California. He has many years of experience helping startup businesses.

I'm not worried because he's been very successful. Believe me, the way he spends money…"

"Soo, were you considering loaning him the money?"

"Well… I decided to borrow it from my IRA. I called my investment guy, and he wasn't too happy about my decision. But I told him I should get it back in a few months."

"OK, wait a minute. So, you offered to loan Steve the money? But you're retired, and that's all the money you've got. Isn't he the same age too?"

"Yes he is, but we're married now and Steve said we share our income and expenses. Luckily, my house is almost paid off. The thing is that I used to take care of myself, especially when I was getting alimony from my ex. But now I depend on Steve. I know I shouldn't worry because he makes sure I have everything I need."

"Now that you brought this up, it's an interesting situation at our age, being retired and living on a fixed income. When my husband at the time and I were married and raising a family, it was a given to share income and expenses. But one thing I made perfectly clear is that I'd pay the bills and what was left over was to save or for play money."

"I was the same way in my previous marriage of thirty-two years. I don't see there's any difference here. When you get married, don't you think you share the income and expenses?"

"It didn't occur to me until having this conversation. It's a great question. Okay, so I'm retired too, approaching 70 and not planning on getting married again. But if I loaned money from my retirement fund to let's say my hypothetical husband, and he lost it…. The idea of getting a job at my age to survive kind of makes me ill. OK, to answer your question, I wouldn't loan him the money."

"You wouldn't?"

"No! If he's been a successful consultant, I assume he'd have other resources. What if Steve needs more money, would you be willing to loan it to him?"

"Oh… I don't think it would come to that. Steve was in long-term consulting jobs with a super reputation. I also

know he's involved in two business partnerships. Money doesn't seem to be an issue in his extravagant lifestyle."

———— *October 2015* ————

"Hello, Brenda. How are you?"

"Hey, Laura. I'm doing fine. I wanted to say again how much I appreciated your making it to our wedding reception after your pneumonia scare in May. How are you feeling?"

"I'm getting better every day. Still on oxygen at night, but not during the day. Even though your home is at a lower elevation than mine, I still needed oxygen at night when I came to your reception."

"I didn't know you were still on oxygen! You looked beautiful and hid it well."

"Thank you, but I was fading fast towards evening. Greg and I had to leave early, and he took me back to his sister's to hook me up again."

"Oh, you were worse than I thought!"

"My lung doctor asked if I ever considered moving from my house on top of the mountain. I just laughed because I love living in the mountains and have always been very healthy. Although, I expected to recover much faster."

"Yes, but if Greg hadn't taken you to the hospital, you could have died. It's bad enough that you moved away from me and then you almost died!"

"Yeah, I was really lucky he took me there in time. Pneumococcal pneumonia can take you fast if you don't get the correct antibiotic. Hey, how are your girls and grandchildren?"

"They're doing great! Both little families come over for Sunday dinner almost every week. They love Steve and he's so good with the little ones."

"How nice to have them live near you. I wish my children and grandchildren lived near me. But it's difficult when my daughter lives in western Canada and my son lives on the East Coast."

"I am truly blessed. By the way, Steve and I did our Wills together. It was kind of interesting as I set mine up for the kids to inherit a certain percentage of my assets. Steve would get a certain percentage and he'd still live in my house. But the stipulation being that when he dies, the house goes to them."

"Sounds fair to me."

"But he wrote in his Will that just about everything goes to me. I thought it was odd that he left nothing for his two adult kids. We even took out life insurance policies on each other."

"Whoa! It seems a little early to be talking about Wills. At least I think so. When did the idea to do your Wills together come up?"

"Oh, we did them this summer soon after our wedding. Did you ever do a Will with your husband?"

"My first husband and I never talked about a Will as we could barely survive working and raising a family. In my second marriage, when my kids were older and out of the house, I created a Will, specifically with them in mind. It was in self-defense because I came into that marriage with a successful business. My second husband had his dental practice, but he kept making poor business decisions. He even got a second mortgage on our house to cover the business partnerships that failed. You know, it does seem odd that Steve didn't leave anything for his kids."

"Yeah, I thought so too. Later I asked him to explain. He said he was leaving all of his money to me, but there was an exception with his house. Since his house is paid off, it would go to them."

"Hey, wait a minute. You just said Steve's house was paid off. Why didn't he get an equity line of credit on his house to pay the attorney $30,000?"

"Oh, I don't know. I guess we didn't think about it."

—— *February 2016* ——

"Hi, Laura!"

"Hey, Brenda. I hope this is a good time for you. What are you up to?"

"This is perfect! Just chopping up vegetables for a crock pot recipe for dinner tonight."

"I'll make it quick because I don't want to interrupt your concentration. I know when I'm cooking, it takes my full attention.

"Not me. I just follow the directions, throw everything in and add one can of cream of mushroom soup, which seems to make them all delicious... or cream of celery soup."

"That sounds yummy. I'll have to try that sometime. Anyway, I just wanted to thank you again for letting me stay with you last week. So fun getting to know Steve a little better, seeing our old friends and taking care of business."

"Laura! You're always welcome to stay with me! It was great to see you too! Just remember the guest room is there for you anytime."

"That's so sweet. Hey, the dinner that Steve prepared for Saturday night was amazing! He sure knows his wines because I didn't even get a headache."

"Yep, I'd say he's a connoisseur in that department. He loves to cook, and I have no problem with him taking over the kitchen."

"It's obvious he adores you. It sounds like he knows how to take care of you too. From what you told me, you've always been the caretaker. Maybe it's time for a little pampering?"

"Yeah, it sure is a nice change. When I was 16, my father was in a major automobile accident and I'd have to go straight home after school to help my mother with him. It disabled him for years. When I was in college I'd have to help on weekends. Many years after my father passed away, I moved my mother here and got her set up in a little condo close by."

"Oh, Brenda, that must have been difficult!"

"Yeah, it was at times, but you do what you have to do. Hey, I have to tell you Steve makes me feel very special. I've never had anyone wait on me the way he does."

"Like what?"

"Well, for example, before he leaves in the morning, he'll bring me coffee when I'm just waking up. He'll leave little notes around to remind me how much he loves me. And if he gets home early, he'll pick up a steak to grill. He loves grilling vegetables with his special oils and spices, or he'll whip up a gourmet dinner, just like that."

"Lucky you! And I noticed the beautiful flower arrangement on the dining room table."

"Oh yes, he does make sure there are fresh flowers every couple of weeks."

"Wow! Sooo… does he have a brother?"

"Well, if he had one as kind as Steve, I'd definitely introduce you."

"Did you say you met him on Match?"

"Yeah, that's right. I thought I'd try it out. I met a couple of guys from the website, but nobody I was interested in. Steve posted his profile photo, taken in Paris. And that's what attracted me because I love to travel. We emailed back and forth until he asked me out for a drink. He was sitting at the bar when I arrived."

"Did he have his tam on backwards? That's so cool."

"Yep, and I like the way he dresses too. He was easy to talk to and shared interesting stories about his international travels. I liked the way he made me laugh a lot. When we stood up to leave, it surprised me to see he was barely my height of 5'4". His profile on Match said he was 5'6". Since I wasn't looking for a committed relationship at the time, I got over his shortness.

"But he ended up winning your heart after all, right?"

"Yeah, he continues to surprise me with his thoughtfulness. Like last Friday, for example, I met a few girlfriends for Happy Hour and as we were walking out of the bar, he shows up with a gift bag. He was coming to meet me for dinner. Anyway, he saw a dress in the window of a nearby boutique, and said he knew it would look great on me."

"That's awesome! I love hearing about gift giving just for the fun of it. Brenda, you mentioned Steve hasn't moved in yet because he keeps his home office at his house. Is that working out okay?"

"Yes, he makes his business calls from there, so he can write off the expenses on his taxes. He leaves in the morning just about every day during the week and returns for dinner. And then sometimes he's away on business."

"You know, I think you have the best of both worlds. You get used to your own space when you live alone for a while. How do you spend your time now that you're an old married woman?"

"You are so funny! My days are quite busy. When I'm not helping with my grandchildren, I'm still doing photography for a greeting card company, taking painting lessons, or meeting with friends at the social club."

"I've seen some of your photos on the greeting cards. You're incredibly talented! Does Steve like the living arrangements?"

"It seems to be working out. I think he likes it too because he was single for a long time. Sometimes we'll stay at his house, which is only an hour away. But we prefer to spend the weekends here because my house is bigger and close to town with lots going on. Just the other day, he called from our favorite restaurant and said he ordered my special wine and just needed me there to complete his perfect day."

———— *End of March 2016* ————

"Hello, my friend."

"Hey, Laura! It was so nice of you to be available at the last minute to take care of Chester for a few days when Steve and I had to fly to Houston for another job interview."

"Oh, Brenda, it was my pleasure. I've been telling my friends how well trained and sweet Chester is. Even though he's a big golden retriever who could easily pull me down the street, he walked right by my side. One time there was a deer standing off in the trees. Chester saw her too, but he didn't leave my side. What a guy!"

"I know he's a real joy in my life."

"And the best part of the story is the going to bed routine. You told me that when I was ready for bed, I was to say to Chester, 'Last call,' and he'd head for the doggie door in the laundry room, go out to the back yard, do his business, and come right back in."

"You're right. He's such a good boy."

"So, what's happened since I saw you last month?"

"Steve's daughter came to visit. She usually stays at his house so she can visit her neighborhood friends and then comes here for dinner."

"Oh, that's right. I remember you telling me she was going to visit soon. I'm curious how it went."

"She is such a sweetie. We get along just fine."

"Well, you're so easy to get along with, anyway. I'm not surprised."

"She tries to come home on some weekends because she loves our Sunday family dinners with my two daughters and their husbands, kids and dogs! She told me she was glad to see her father happy, and she hopes to be the best aunt ever."

"Oh, Brenda, how wonderful for you! And how about Steve's ex-wife, is she in the background or does she get involved since she lives in the area?"

"Just once so far. She came by to pick up their daughter to take her to lunch one afternoon. She seems nice and told

me how happy she was to know her daughter is part of our family. She isn't at all what I expected, even though Steve isn't one to say unkind things about anyone. He did say that when they were married, she had serious drinking problems and was in and out of rehab a couple of times. I guess she's got her act together now. However, his daughter is much closer to him."

"Oh, and why is that?"

"One time when we flew to New York City to celebrate her birthday, he had special wine and flowers delivered. It astounded me how he spoils her with expensive gifts. They are extremely close. I mean, she calls him almost every day on her way home from work."

"He sounds like he's a caring father too."

"Well, yes, but I was a little concerned about the expensive gifts and I asked him about it. He said he felt guilty about the divorce and her not having a close relationship with her mother. He tries to make up for it. He was a single dad for a while when his wife was in rehab and then after their divorce. From what I've seen, he's very close to his son as well, even cosigned on both kids' college loans."

"Wow, quite a generous dad too."

"Yep. Did I ever tell you how he proposed to me after we dated for a year?"

"I remember you telling me about the first proposal but not sure what changed your mind."

"You know how much I love France since my daughter had a job in Paris and eventually married a Frenchman? She ended up living there for seven years before they moved here. When they started having children, I, of course, had to visit them to see my grandchildren. They're so adorable and he's the best husband and father. I used to spend a month in June and rent a little place close by. I had to brush up on my French just so I could talk to my grandchildren. Anyway, I thought it might be fun for Steve and I to visit them. Since he traveled internationally for business, he upgraded our tickets to First Class."

"Now that's the way to go, especially when you fly to France!"

"Yep! I'm telling you just about everything we do is First Class. Anyway, one afternoon when we were touring around Paris, we stopped for lunch at a little café and

that's where he proposed to me. But I said, 'No.' It seemed too soon, since we only dated for a year. You know how much I didn't want to get married. I just wasn't ready to feel trapped again."

"Right, I remember. That's why it amazed me that you changed your mind."

"Well, a year later, we were on a business trip to Vegas. He arranged for us to stay at the penthouse of this fancy hotel. So, while we were having dinner at this very romantic restaurant, he proposed to me again. And so… I said, 'Yes.' The timing just seemed right. Don't you think? I mean, being with someone for two years, you should know each other pretty well by then?"

"I would think so. Even though yours is a committed relationship, I still question why he was so persistent about getting married. Although you are a pretty savvy, independent woman. I don't understand why people with adult children feel they need to get married in their mid-sixties or older. I suppose it can be financially advantageous or for religious reasons, which I do respect. It definitely gets more complicated as we get older."

PART II
The Victim

– Fast Forward Two Years to March 2018 –

"Hello, Brenda, how are ya?"

"Hey, Laura, you won't believe what's happening. I got this call from a debt consolation company saying I owed over $10,000 on a credit card with over $500 in late fees!"

"Yikes! That's scary!"

"They called last month, but I thought it was a scam call, and I just ignored it. After Steve finally moved in, some questionable things started happening that got my attention."

"Right, I remember you telling me about his moving in and setting up his office in one of your guest rooms. Renting his house out was a smart idea. Even better, since he said it was paid off. OK, so what kind of questionable things are happening?"

"One day while he was away, I was looking for a paperclip in his desk drawers. Well, you know me, I'm not one to snoop into someone's private things, but I saw several credit cards with an elastic band around them. You won't

believe what I found. There were fourteen credit cards and some of them had Steve's kids' names on them. Then I found a letter from a debt relief company saying his consolidation loan for $127,000 was paid. I took photos of everything."

"It sounds like Steve had more debt than you thought when you guys met. You poor thing! Do you think he might have gotten an equity loan on his house to pay off that debt?"

"Yeah, I think it's very possible."

"So maybe that's why he told you he hadn't thought about getting a line of credit, because there probably wasn't any equity left, right?"

"Absolutely! And you know, thinking back I just remembered Steve wanting me to get a credit card a few months after we were married. He suggested that I could get miles on this one, even though I didn't need one. He seems to know about these things better than I do. Do you think this is the same credit card?"

"It's possible!"

"He could have seen my password when I was setting it up. I don't want to think he would stoop that low. Maybe it's time for me to ask him some questions about all of this. I'm sure he can explain."

"Brenda, I just got an idea. How about doing a little research before you have this conversation? What do you think about going to the county clerk's office and looking up his property address? Find out if there is a line of credit or any liens on it."

——— *Mid-March 2018* ———

"Hello, Brenda, what did you find out?"

"Well, it's very complicated since the address is in a town which shares two different counties, and they haven't kept the records up to date. But I found out he did get a second mortgage for $127,000.

"Are you thinking what I'm thinking?"

"Yep! He used it to pay off the credit card debt. And get this! He's still paying on his first mortgage. He never paid it off, as he told me more than once!"

"That's crazy! Maybe, since their records aren't totally up to date, we shouldn't jump to conclusions about the first mortgage. Did it show that the $127,000 was ever paid?"

"No, nothing there. I'm feeling sick about all of this. I finally called my oldest daughter to come over, and I told her what I discovered. She was kind of hurt because I hadn't confided in her sooner. It has been hard to share any of this because she really likes Steve and so do my grandchildren. Anyway, she suggested I have this meeting with him outside of the house, maybe at a hotel bar."

"Brenda, I'm so sorry you have to go through this. It's a good thing you told your daughter. Don't you think she understands why you held back telling her?"

"I didn't confide in any of my friends or family about this except for you. I'm so grateful for our friendship and wish you were here, but at least we can talk on the phone."

"You know you can call me anytime."

"Now that I told my daughter, I feel better about her knowing. Even though we are very close, I just didn't want her to worry. You know how we don't want to burden our adult children when they have enough to worry about taking care of a family, and she and her husband juggling jobs."

"I totally understand, but you know I'm here for you, and I appreciate your catching me up on the questionable details. By the way, I've been curious how the $700,000 theft investigation was progressing. Since you didn't mention it before, I didn't want to pry. You're amazing how you can appear so happy and jovial. And all this time, you've been carrying a tremendous amount of stress."

"You're right there! I kept thinking Steve knew what he was doing. He always seemed calm and confident. That's Steve, always calm. I've never seen him get angry about anything. You'd think he would show some frustration, but I never saw it. He was very persistent on making calls, doing his research on potential opportunities for his next consulting job."

"Did you ever see any evidence that the $700,000 theft was for real, you know, like a document or a letter from the law firm or the investment company he was dealing with?"

"He told me he was in touch with the FBI, and they thought it might be mob related. I was so trusting and never thought to ask for any records, but eventually I did. He gave me copies of emails he received from the secretary at the investment company giving him updates. I think her name was Ester something. He also gave me an email from the attorney's office, which I can't remember the name right now. So that satisfied my curiosity and didn't feel I needed to ask any further."

———— *Late March 2018* ————

"Hello, Brenda, I'm glad you called. You've been on my mind, and I wondered how your meeting with Steve went."

"Well… we met at a local seafood bar that we like, and he thought it was just a casual dining out. I was so nervous about meeting him with all my suspicions, and you know how I hate confrontations."

"Yeah, I know, I'm the same way."

"I started out telling him about receiving a call from the debt consolidation company asking about the credit card with my name on it. His answer was, 'they must have been mistaken.' Then I told him I was looking in his desk drawers for a paperclip when I discovered the fourteen credit cards. I apologized, saying I didn't mean to look further, but I noticed three of the cards had his kids' names on them. He said, 'it's not uncommon to have several credit cards when you own your own business to take care of the slow times.' He said he always paid them off and was quite proud of not having to get a loan. It was no big deal to him."

"What about the letter from the debt relief company?"

"He said he didn't tell me about it because he didn't want me to worry, and that his number one goal was to take care of me. He apologized for all the confusion and said he could fix everything."

"Oh, Brenda! How did you hold it together when you're getting suspicious and he's calm and cool with his answers?"

"You can imagine I'm in shock, confused, and yet wanting to trust him. Just the same, when we got home, I pulled up this credit card in question on my computer and showed it to him. He said he thought it was his! Can you believe that? We both could see my name was on it. That's when I knew he was lying. I felt like I needed a cigarette and I don't even smoke."

"Brenda, this all seems so bizarre! I mean the fact that he calmly tells you it's no big deal."

"At that moment, I knew I couldn't handle him living here, especially with growing suspicions of his lying to me... so calmly. I thought I might ask him to leave in a couple of weeks to give me time to get more answers."

"Sounds like a smart plan."

"I managed to ask him about the second mortgage. He answered that question kind of nonchalantly. He said that when he explained it to me before, I probably didn't remember because of a few too many drinks. I was sort of shocked he said it like that, because I don't drink that much, right?"

"Absolutely not! So, I'm guessing he didn't try to explain it to you again?"

"No, he didn't. And I was too embarrassed, so I didn't push it."

"What's your plan then?"

"Well… there is more to the story about my giving him $30,000 at the start of this $700,000 fraud, which I never told you about."

"Oh?"

"I know you advised me, if you were in my shoes, you wouldn't even loan him the money. The point you made, and I didn't listen, is the difference between retired

individuals and young newlyweds sharing income and expenses. Well, I was just married and fully trusting Steve's business sense, so I decided to get a line of credit from my IRA. My investment guy was freaking out and advised against it and...."

"Wait a minute. The last I heard you were going to loan him $30,000 to pay the attorney fees, and now you're telling me you got a line of credit from your IRA?"

"Yep, and it gets worse! Good old trusting me shows Steve the checkbook connected to the line of credit, and I told him he could write himself a $30,000 check. I looked at the checkbook a few days later and noticed he wrote two checks for $30,000. I questioned him about it, and he thought it was OK, since he'd already told me about one of his businesses going south. That rubbed me wrong. So, I told him he needed to ask me first before writing any checks from now on."

"It's a wonder he didn't use the excuse again about your drinking too much and not remembering. Pardon my sarcasm, but it's beginning to sound like he's taking advantage of you."

"Yeah, right? But when he had a job, he'd ask me what I needed for bills for that month. He immediately wrote

me a check for $5,000. No questions asked. When the money was there, he was always very generous."

"I'm afraid to ask, but how much have you taken from your IRA to loan him so far?"

"Are you ready for this? Maybe you should sit down. He's taken $150,000 so far!"

"Yikes! No way! I can't imagine how you kept this all to yourself."

"There was a lot of personal stuff going on then with my cousin dying from cancer and then a wonderful friend of mine landed in the hospital for a long time, because they couldn't figure out what was causing her stomach pain. I visited her almost every day and helped take care of a few of her business matters. I also had a serious talk with her two daughters because they seemed too busy with their personal lives to visit their mother more often. And when we weren't home, I was traveling with Steve for business meetings. While he was in his meetings, he'd suggest I enjoy sitting by the pool or spend a day at the spa."

"Oh, Brenda! It sounds like he still treated you to the first-class lifestyle to keep up the facade when, in fact, he was charging up a storm."

"The two years of courting and the first year of marriage were loads of fun with the traveling and the high life. I met some of his friends and business colleagues and they all raved about him."

"I can certainly see where you'd be impressed by his grand lifestyle and his friends confirming what a great guy he was."

"OK, so here's what I did after my suspicions were confirmed. I felt really sick thinking the man I loved was lying and stealing from me. After about a week of trying to act normal, I was out running errands, and it hit me that I had to do something. I just couldn't be in the same house with Steve, or even in the same room for one more week. I called him and was mortified, asking him to leave because I needed some space. He immediately said, 'I'll be gone in an hour.' It didn't matter to me where he was going since his house was rented out. When he left, he only took his medications and some clothes, probably thinking he'd be coming back soon."

"Wow, that took a lot of courage to ask him to leave."

"Now you can understand where I'm coming from. I feel so sad when I think of how I believed him, and yet he was always so calm through this whole thing. I didn't talk to anyone about it because he'd say everything will be all right. In the last couple of months, he transferred cash of two $5,000 checks to his checking account. And, get this, an $800 check to pay for a business conference that he previously told me was paid by the company interested in hiring him."

"He must think you have a poor memory as well as a drinking problem."

"Very funny! But it felt so good to be taken care of by Steve. I made myself avoid any red flags that were hitting me over the head."

"You shouldn't be so hard on yourself. You know when love gets in the mix, sometimes we lose ourselves."

"Here's something else that happened that made me ask him to leave. About six months ago, he took out $40,000 to pay for his expenses."

"Brenda, that's a lot of money! Did you ask what it was for?"

"I guess at the time, his answer made sense."

"It sounds like he's getting desperate. You do realize that while you're married to Steve, you're responsible for any debts he's accumulated."

—————— *Mid-April 2018* ——————

"Hello, Brenda, how are ya?"

"Laura, I hope you don't mind my calling so late, but I need to talk to you about a decision I have to make. I've been so anxious about all of this."

"Geez, Brenda, you know you can call me anytime. You've had a lot going on and so much to process. Tell me what's happening?"

"I was thinking back to our earlier conversation when you mentioned I would be liable for Steve's debts because we're married. I'm seriously considering getting a divorce."

"Has something else happened?"

"You know, I should be journaling this stuff so I can keep track of the lies. For example, before I asked him to leave, he came home with a brand-new BMW. You can imagine I'm literally looking at him and the car with my mouth wide open about to say…. you know what!"

"You mean like WTF?!!!"

"Oh my god!!! It's a wonder I don't have high blood pressure. Maybe I do. Who knows?"

"So, what did he say?"

"Apparently… to him the lease on his old BMW ended, and it was time to trade it in. He said he was good buddies with the owner of the dealership, and he was giving him a great deal. I told him it didn't make sense. And why couldn't he lease a less expensive car? He said for me not to worry because his veteran's disability check of $400 a month would pay for it."

"Really? This is worse than I thought. I didn't realize he was getting disability checks. For what?"

"He had a serious leg injury when he was in Vietnam. It bothers him occasionally, but it didn't stop him when we played Pickleball!"

"Hmm, that's interesting, I never noticed that he had a limp."

"His debts seem to continue and so do his lies."

"So, what do you have in mind?"

"I'm thinking of calling the divorce attorney I used when I filed for divorce from my first husband of thirty-two years. She is what you'd call a Bulldog Attorney. She was exactly what I needed at that time because my ex was being so difficult and hateful. Even though we met before he started med school, I helped to support him all through school and even set up his practice. I managed his business and our personal finances for years. When we adopted our first child nine years later, I continued to manage everything part time. Then, my mother was getting ill, and I had to take her to doctor appointments. You get it, right?"

"Right. Sounds like you had your hands full, to say the least."

"Anyway, my involvement in growing his business was definitely a partnership, and he didn't want to give me anything in the divorce. The attorney arranged for a decent settlement in the beginning, and the rest paid off as alimony checks."

"That sounds fair. I'm curious why you got a divorce."

"In the last few years of our marriage, he had a serious drinking problem and could become verbally abusive

when he got drunk. Even now when we attend family events with our kids, he just scowls at me and he still blames me for ruining his life. Unfortunately, he hasn't stopped drinking and I think his practice is suffering."

"I don't know how you could do it all, eventually raising three kids and taking care of your mother at the same time. It's a shame that he still blames you. Good thing you don't have to see him very often. I suppose you're able to put on a happy face for the kids."

"They seem to understand his moods. Sometimes I fear for my life, though. He owns a gun which he keeps in his car, and who knows if he gets drunk and decides to threaten me."

"What makes you think he'd do something like that? Was he ever physically abusive with you?"

"Yeah, not many people know this. One time he got drunk and really mean, pushing me around, and that did it! I made him move out. He was gone for a year, but he was a good father and still did things with the kids, you know, like attending all their events. Since he seemed to get his act together and the kids missed him being home, I agreed to have him move back."

"In other words, you allowed him to move back for the kids, but it sounds like he continued to drink."

"When the kids were out of the house and away at college, he got worse again. That's when I got the divorce. I don't know, I can't figure him out. We've been divorced for eight years and every time we see each other at these family events, he just seems to resent me even more."

"Oh, I'm so sorry you have to deal with that kind fear in the midst of deciding what to do about Steve. Have you heard from him?"

"He sends a text or an email every couple of days saying how much he loves me and wants to take care of me. He's sorry things kind of got out of hand, but he's hoping we can work it out."

"He said he's sorry that things kind of got out of hand?"

"Oh yeah, and he said that when his retirement fund is recovered, he'd share it with me. Sometimes I wish this was just a bad dream."

"Do you respond to him?"

"No, I can't give him any encouragement. I vacillate between feeling betrayed and angry and then missing him. I mean, his kids adore him, and his friends think he's the best. How can you argue with that? But when I look back at all the lies and the red flags I ignored, it gives me the courage and determination to do what I have to do."

"I can see how this could wear you down."

"You know when I met him, I had no debt except for the house mortgage. I was receiving a nice rental income from the one-bedroom apartment in the basement. The guy I rented it to is a friend of my daughter's, very trustworthy, and he even took care of Chester when I went away. My dog loved him too."

"Did you continue to rent it out after you guys got married?"

"About six months after we were married, Steve didn't want anyone in the house. In fact, he bought a big screen TV and put it downstairs in that apartment. Even though we had one in the living room and in our bedroom. He said he liked it down there, in particular on those hot summer days."

"Well, it sounds like you've made up your mind."

———— *Mid-May 2018* ————

"Hey, Laura."

"Hi Brenda, just thought I'd check up on you. Is this a good time to talk?"

"Perfect! Chester and I are enjoying this beautiful day. Our walks seem to take longer every time because we're meeting more new friends at the park. He's getting to be quite popular! My neighbor even likes to take him for a walk with his dog because they've become pals."

"That's a good one. Are you sure your neighbor isn't wanting you to go on the walks too?"

"You're so funny. Of course not! Hey, I do have some good news."

"Great! I'm ready to hear some good news."

"I have an appointment with my attorney in two weeks. I was so lucky because she's getting ready to retire."

"Fabulous! I guess you were serious!"

"Yep, when I make up my mind, look out!"

"I can believe that. Have you heard from Steve?"

"Well, every day there's a new discovery. Steve has been filing our joint tax returns, and it occurred to me that I hadn't seen the tax returns from the last couple of years. When I was single, I always did it myself, but it sure was nice to have him take care of it. I guess I just let it slide because there was so much other stuff to be concerned about. Anyway, I asked him for a copy of our tax returns a few months ago. He said he would get them from his accountant. Then it turned into a complicated mess because he said the secretary couldn't find the right pages. To make a long story short, he didn't even use an accountant. He did it on Turbo Tax. He said we got money back, which I never saw. The lies just keep pouring out with a smile and a gentle nature. OK, enough about me. How are you doing in your new home?"

"But wait before I answer that question. Did you ever get a copy of your tax returns?"

"Yes, he finally gave me a copy of last year's. That's how I discovered he used Turbo Tax. I'm still waiting to see copies of the previous years."

"OK, to answer your question. Yes, I do love it here in northwest Montana, living at a lower elevation which makes my lungs happy, and still have mountains close by. Best of all, I'm only a six-hour drive to visit my daughter and grandchildren in Canada. Now that I'm retired, I can see them more often. You're very lucky to have your grandchildren close by."

"Yeah, I love it. They are a joy in my life. When my daughters' need me to babysit, I'm there. My little French grandchildren crack me up because they'll eat anything we cook, which is not typical for most little ones. I love being with them. But to be perfectly honest, most of the time I feel like a zombie, putting on a cheerful face when I feel like I could throw up."

"Brenda, I wonder if other women have had similar experiences. You know, like finding out their husband lied about his net worth and ended up taking theirs."

"I swear, you and I have like minds. As a matter of fact, I happened to google lying about money in marriage, and this is what I found. Let me get it so I can read part of it to you. 'Financial infidelity is more common than you think, and it varies from hiding credit card debt, holding secret accounts, lying about net worth, hiding gambling

or shopping addictions.' The article went on to say that 'financial infidelity is outright lying and can be toxic to the relationship.' It certainly contributed to trust issues in our marriage."

"Isn't it interesting there's a name for it? I never heard of it before. I mean, we've all heard about sexual infidelity but not financial infidelity."

"It said it usually starts out innocently, like wanting to avoid an argument, especially if the couple has differing money management habits. That's us for sure. When I realized our debt was accumulating, I suggested we should create a budget. When I asked him to give me a budget for his house, he didn't include his unpaid back taxes or credit card debts or the two mortgages on his house."

"You know, Brenda, that reminds me of a friend's experience. He was 65 and divorced for a long time. He said a buddy of his talked him into joining an online dating site for people who belonged to his religion. The guys decided to find someone with the same beliefs. My friend met a lady about his age who lived in the next state. So, he flew to visit her in his small private plane and since they were quite impressed with each other, got married six months later in Vegas."

"You've got to be kidding! Married in Vegas?"

"Well, he was getting pretty lonely living in a small town. He had a beautiful home on a lake, though."

"You're saying they got married after six months of dating?"

"Kind of sounds like it, right? Anyway, she sold her house, at least that's what she said, and moved in with him. She wanted to renovate his house with an addition. Since he was in love with this rare piece of humanity, he agreed and ended up with an architect's bill of $8,000. She wanted to put her name on the deed of his house, which led to other demands. After eight months of this, he began to recognize her real personality as a mean and nasty shrew. And those are his exact words. I'm guessing she was impressed with his airplane lifestyle, which actually was his passion. But in reality, he was very frugal and lived simply. Somehow she got a different impression."

"But how much can you know about a person in six months?"

"Correct! In the divorce settlement, it required him to pay her a certain amount of money that she said she lost through their marriage. Get this. A couple of years later, he discovered she deceived a previous husband in a short-term marriage for a lot more money."

"There! See, it can happen to anyone!"

———— *Late May 2018* ————

"Hey Brenda, I'm so glad you called because I'm curious how the appointment went with your attorney."

"First of all, I thanked her for squeezing me in so quickly. I told her all about the $700,000 theft of Steve's retirement fund and my loaning him $150,000 from my IRA. I still can't believe I did that! Anyway, I told her about all the other lies. During our appointment, she looked over the papers I gave her and then asked me what I wanted to do. I told her I didn't want to be liable for any of his debt. She said she would take care of it. She advised me to tell Steve that we both have an appointment with her next Friday and that she will make things right."

"Wow, she works fast!"

"One reason is we're hoping he still has equity left in his house to pay me off. He's been renting his house out, which he uses to pay his expenses. I was the one who found the renter for him. I called the renter's boss to confirm he made enough money to pay the rent."

———— Early June 2018————

"Hi Brenda, how are you doing?"

"Sort of OK. How are you?"

"I'm doing fine, thank you. I'm visiting my daughter for a week, and I love living closer to her and the grandkids. The six-hour drive over the Canadian border isn't really that bad either. OK, enough about me. I want to hear how the meeting went with you and Steve and your attorney."

"Actually, I'm still shaking even though the meeting was yesterday. I feel like I've been on a rollercoaster ride this past year, and I'm worried something else will blow up in my face. It seems surreal, this whole thing, even the meeting with the attorney."

"When you think about what you've been through, it's understandable you feel the way you do. It's fortunate that your children are supportive, that is, if you let them."

"Yeah, well, I don't want them to worry about me. It doesn't feel right, but I appreciate you saying that. Anyway, back to

the meeting. Basically, she will represent me in court and file for an annulment which would totally protect me from any of Steve's debts."

"Hey, did you say an annulment? I thought it was almost impossible to get one."

"I thought so too, but when it comes to financial infidelity and lying about net worth before marriage, it's possible. I'm glad she knows what she's doing. She emphasized that Steve will have to sell his house and the amount we will ask for is $200,000."

"Wow! How did it get to $200,000?"

"She figures he owes me the $150,000 from my IRA, the $15,000 credit card debt, and some of my monthly alimony that I lost when I married him. She put my name on the deed of his house in case it doesn't sell in six months, then I'd have control of selling it. You know the strange part of all of this was that Steve was his cool and calm self, very nice. He signed all the documents without questions. She told us at the beginning of the meeting that it was being recorded. So, when she asked him if his house was paid off, he said yes. Can you believe that? He lied, and it was recorded!"

—— *Mid-June 2018* ——

"Hello, Brenda! Great to hear from you. What's happening?"

"I need to find a realtor and I remember hearing you talk about the one you used when you were flipping houses."

"Yep, I can help you there, but why do you need one? Are you selling your house too?"

"Oh, no, no. After the meeting with the attorney, Steve realized he'd have to sell his house soon because the lease is up for the present renters and new ones are moving in on July 1st."

"July 1st? That's only two weeks away!"

"Yeah, I know. Luckily, they haven't signed a lease yet. He notified the young couple to tell them he had to sell the house. They were very disappointed, but then told him they might be able to buy it."

"That's encouraging."

"Well, it turns out there were some complications. The young husband's father was going to make the down payment for them, but he discovered his son had huge credit card debt and reneged. Sound familiar? Another liar for ya! Then the young wife's mother stepped in and offered to help. Isn't that interesting? You know, I think couples who plan to marry ought to have an Experian party to check each other's credit rating."

"What a great idea! I think you're right. How many couples do you know actually do background checks or confirm financial stability? Once you get intimate in a relationship, sometimes you lose yourself in wanting it to work and ignore the red flags."

"I think I was doing the same thing, but maybe I waited too long. Hard to say. Because when you're beginning to get suspicious, you also doubt yourself. What made it difficult for me was Steve being so kind and caring. He was like my best friend. We enjoyed the same TV shows and watched sports together. Remember how I loved playing Pickleball? He learned to play, and we also played golf together on several weekends."

"I can see where he made you feel very special."

"He was the Rock of Gibraltar for me. Believe me, I had enough drama going on in my life. He gave great advice and big hugs."

"I understand how tough this must be for you… vacillating back and forth can certainly wear you down."

"You're right there. I so appreciate our friendship and being able to talk to you about all of this. By the way, I remember you telling me about the realtor you worked with when you were flipping houses after moving here. If the approval goes through with the bank, all Steve needs is a realtor to create the documents for the sale. Didn't he sell you your house, too?"

"Yes, in the fall of 2007, Sam and I must have looked at 20 different places in less than a week when I was in town. After I got settled, he was like a mentor to me when I decided to invest in foreclosed houses to renovate and flip. He owns several rentals and also flipped houses. I was lucky to have his expert advice. Even his wife gave me the best renovation tips. Yep, Sam's your man. I'll email an introduction to you both."

—————— *Mid-July 2018* ——————

"Hello, Brenda, how are you?"

"Hey, Laura, I'm doing much better. I wanted to thank you so much for recommending Sam to take care of the paperwork for the house sale. It's in the works now, and it looks like the young couple will buy it."

"That's fantastic news! It will be interesting to see what the net profit brings after Steve pays off the mortgages."

"We shall see. OK, are you sitting down because you're not going to like what I'm about to tell you?"

"Oh no, what's happening?"

"Emma, a delightful friend of mine who lives close by, has been inviting me and Steve to join her and her husband to some social events over the past several months. I had to give excuses why we couldn't join them. You know, with all the craziness going on. Anyway, she and I finally met for dinner, and I filled her in on some issues and mentioned the theft of Steve's retirement fund. She was shocked and yet supported me in what I had to do. She

asked if it was OK to tell her husband because he might have suggestions about the theft."

"I'm glad to hear you're reaching out to nearby friends."

"They are the sweetest friends. We had our wedding reception at their home."

"Oh, that's right! I remember them and their lovely home."

"Anyway, they called back and her husband asked if I ever contacted the investment company or Steve's attorney. He asked if it was all right to make those calls."

"Oh, Brenda, what a nice guy to offer to call them."

"Emma's husband called both Steve's attorney and the investment company. They never heard of Steven Chadberg nor the secretary who supposedly sent Steve the emails!"

"What?! This is worse than I thought! Are you saying the whole thing was a lie? But what about the emails he showed you from his attorney and the investment company?"

"Emma said it was a cut-and-paste job, which apparently is easy to do."

"Oh, no! Does that mean Steve lied from the beginning? I just don't understand how someone can be loving and attentive all these years and yet continue to borrow or steal, whatever you want to call it."

"Tell me about it. I'm still trying to wrap my head around this whole thing. Makes me wonder who Steve really is."

"I felt I was a good judge of character when first meeting people. You know how you can tell right off if you can trust them? Like meeting a friend of a friend at a party, and he touches your arm each time when he makes a point, which he assumes you both agree on. Or the charming fellow that you wish to move away from ASAP. Honestly, Steve doesn't fit any of those characteristics. Sorry, Brenda, but I didn't see him as the charming type."

"Well, he did have his ways."

—————— *Early August 2018* ——————

"Hello, Brenda, how are you?"

"Hey, Laura, I'm okay, I guess, under the circumstances. You know what makes this whole annulment so difficult? Steve keeps sending emails about how much he loves me and feels we can still work this out. Can you believe that?"

"I can believe it. He doesn't want to lose you."

"In his recent email, he said he was in a state of shock after meeting with the attorney. He had no idea about the annulment being discussed and was devastated with how he responded to her question about the house. Oh yeah, and get this. He proposed a deal at the closing of the house sale to hold back about $60,000 which he'd pay me later. Really?!! Do you think that's going to happen? Then he ends the email saying, 'being with you in these past years has been the best ever in my life.'"

"When you discovered all his debts and lies, did you ever discuss going to counseling?"

"About a year ago, I brought it up when our living expenses were increasing. He felt jobs would come in soon and said

when you own your own business, you have to get creative. It's part of staying in business."

"What you're saying gives me the impression that he didn't feel there was a problem."

"Right, and the discussion ended there. How can you argue with a man in denial? But soon after our discussion, he got a three-month consulting job down south. That made me question myself and made me wonder if he could bring things around."

"Talk about a rollercoaster ride alright!"

"Yeah, and the contractor wanted him to live there, so he could be on the job to help set up their business. He invited me to spend a couple of weeks with him in this cute little apartment they rented for him. When I arrived, I discovered he bought new sheets and towels, shampoo and creams. He said he wanted it to be perfect. I never had anyone do things like that for me."

"Yeah, I guess you could say he went a little above and way beyond."

"During those three months, he would come home for long weekends, and then I would fly there for a week or

two. We met the contractor for dinner a few times. They would always end up talking business. The contractor was very complimentary and showed a lot of respect for Steve's knowledge and work ethic."

"So, are you having second thoughts about your decision? I mean, your court date is in a couple of weeks."

"Oh, no, no. Here's something else I meant to tell you. Back when I went through his desk drawers and found those fourteen credit cards, I also discovered an old ID with his date of birth making him three years older than he said he was. I asked him about it, and he told me the Air Force messed up on his birth date. So that means he's been collecting Social Security since we married. This past year and a half, not only did he get Social Security, his disability checks, the rent from his house and income from jobs. And I ask you, why did he keep taking money out of my IRA?"

"Good question, Brenda. Hey, when Steve moved in, did he change his address to receive mail at your house?"

"No, he got a post office box in town. Ahhh, oh! I guess I was oblivious to a lot! I might have caught on sooner if his mail was delivered here."

———— *Mid-August 2018* ————

Court Date

"Oh, Brenda, thanks for calling. I've been thinking about you all morning. How are you doing?"

"Laura, you are the first person I'm calling today after the court appearance. Well, I barely made it through the hearing without fainting. I was so nervous. I'm sure I've lost 20 pounds through this whole ordeal and my clothes just hang on me. But I don't care. I just don't care how I look. I'm trying to stay strong though."

"OK, stop for a minute. I can tell you're probably still shaking. Sit down. Are you sitting down?"

"No, I'm standing and pacing."

"Will you please sit down because I want you to take a few deep breaths? I'm so sorry I can't be there to give you support in person. It's quite traumatic to go through something like this. Are you taking some deep breaths?"

"Yeah… OK. I wish you could have been there to witness the lies pouring out of him! He had to fill out a financial

report to give to the judge and to my attorney. One thing I got to see on the report was the payment for his new BMW lease. It was $600 a month, not $400. Then he told the court that his fraternity brother stole his retirement fund along with other fraternity brothers' funds. And here's the strangest part. Steve said the stolen funds were now hidden in an offshore account, and that's why he had to borrow money from me. My attorney advised him not to mention it because she wasn't sure it actually happened. If he wasn't telling the truth, they could charge him with perjury. Big surprise to me about the offshore account. He has complete finesse in lying."

"Any idea why he changed his story?"

"Steve had to submit his assets and liabilities to the court to show he didn't have any assets other than his house. To prove this, he came up with the story about his retirement funds being stolen and in an offshore account."

"If the stolen funds are in an offshore account, how could he possibly know where they are?"

"Bingo! You got it. This just doesn't make sense. I can't understand why the judge didn't question him on how he learned they were offshore."

"Brenda, was the annulment granted during this court appearance?"

"Yes, amazingly! They granted the annulment. However, my attorney had to prove Steve came into the marriage lying about his credit card debt, two mortgages and a debt consolidation loan. She stated that because of the marriage, I lost my alimony payments and then depended on him. He also had to admit that he married me for my money."

"Oh no! He had to admit it in court with you present?"

"Yes! He hesitated before answering the question from my attorney. She told him before entering the court that he'd have to answer that question."

"Do you think he married you for your money?"

"No, I can't believe it's possible. How can you fake a five-year loving relationship?"

"What else happened? How is he supposed to pay you back?"

"He's supposed to pay me the net proceeds from the house sale. Let's hope there's enough left to recoup what I lost."

PART III
The Aftermath

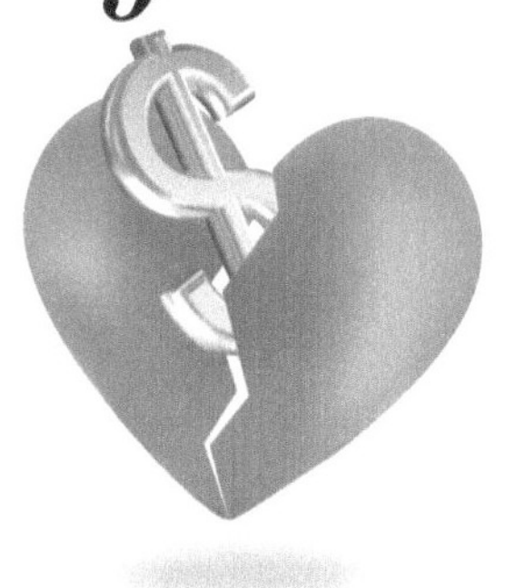

———— *End of August 2018* ————

"Hey."

"Hi Brenda, how are you?"

"I'm okay. Do you remember my telling you Steve emailed me a proposal before the court appearance that he wanted $60,000 when the house sold?"

"Right, I remember you telling me something like that."

"His plan was to have money to live on. Now when I think about it, he kind of threatened that if I didn't agree, he wouldn't show up in court."

"You've got to be kidding! I know you're not kidding, but he has a lot of nerve to push it."

"Oh, yeah, and at the end of one of his recent emails, he says he's lighting candles for me in church every day."

"You're telling me he went to church every morning! Did he go to Mass on Sundays too?"

"When he could. I didn't go with him though. That was his thing. He grew up going to Catholic schools and his grandmother was a big influence on him."

"His religious intentions seem to contradict his lifestyle and lying."

"Right you are there."

"I'm guessing the closing on the house already happened. Was there enough money left for you?"

"After they paid the mortgages, it left me enough to pay off the credit card of $15,000 and the one I had to charge for living expenses of $17,000. I ended up with $115,000. A far cry from what I lost. But according to the annulment agreement, he will have to pay me the balance at $200 a month."

"Hold on a minute. Did you say there were two credit cards to pay off?"

"Yes, when he wasn't getting jobs as often in the last year of our marriage, I wasn't able to pay off my credit card monthly like I used to, which escalated to $17,000 for our living expenses. Let's just not go there, OK?"

———— *Mid-September 2018* ————

"Hello, Brenda. Great to hear from you. How are ya doin'?"

"Hi, Laura, I'm doing OK. I'm just checking to find out if you're still coming to visit at the end of September."

"Oh, yes, absolutely! Now that I made my plane reservations, I can give you a date for my visit. I'm arriving on September 27th. The leaves should be at their peak by then. At least I hope so."

"Perfect, and my guest room is all ready for you! We'll be able to go hiking because the weather should still be warm."

"I'm so looking forward to seeing you and trying some of those fabulous restaurants you told me about."

"Yeah, it should be fun. I met my friend, Marlene, for dinner at this new restaurant for us to check out. Do you remember my telling you about her?"

"Maybe you told me you met her at the social club that we belonged to. Or rather, I used to belong to, until I moved away. But I don't think she was there when I was a member."

"Well, we've known each other for a few years and I always enjoyed meeting her at the club. Sometimes Steve and I would meet Marlene for dinner. In fact, she and Steve met for dinner a couple of times when I was out of town. They loved sharing business stories. She built up this incredible business and later sold it for millions, which allowed her to retire early and travel. Anyway, I met her for dinner the other night because I hadn't seen her in several months. She asked how Steve was doing and, of course, she didn't know what happened. I filled her in on the annulment. I tried to give her very little information without giving her the gory details. It took her by surprise since it seemed to happen so quickly. However, I did mention finding all those credit cards in his desk. Marlene actually defended him because she said it wasn't uncommon when the business income wasn't paying the expenses. Some people might use credit cards to get back on track. She heard of a guy who was so desperate he stole from his mother just to save himself. She liked Steve and knew he would never do anything like that."

"Very interesting that she defended him. How'd that make you feel?"

"Marlene's done well in business and I respect her opinions. Using credit cards to get out of debt or to carry you over might work for some people. But having fourteen credit cards and some with your kids' names on them seems a little suspicious in the legality category, don't you think?"

"Oh yeah, that's serious. But I can understand using a credit card loan to hold you over because I had to resort to that strategy when I was flipping houses."

"You did?"

"Yep, I bought my first foreclosed house in April 2008. Sam recommended a few of his crew to help on this project, and they were great. I was on the job every day as the general contractor. The renovations were completed in a month, and I had a contract on the house a month later."

"Hey, good job!"

"And then Sam suggested another foreclosed house near the same neighborhood. However, my dilemma was not having enough cash to buy it. So, a good friend of mine became my business partner on this one. OK, here's where it gets a little scary. The problems started with the closings. The buyers were approved, but that wasn't the issue. There were so many foreclosed houses being sold that year, the banks didn't have enough people to process the paperwork. At least that's what I was told. I thought I'd done my homework on these two investments, keeping the cost of renovations down, and I felt confident the first house would close sooner. So, having all my cash tied up in these two houses put me in a serious bind, because I couldn't pay the mortgage on my own house."

"Talk about stress, Laura, I don't think I could handle it. I don't remember you mentioning this to me."

"It's not the kind of social conversation I wanted to share with anyone. So, this is what I did. My credit card company kept sending me blank checks to borrow up to $10,000 at 1.99% for a year. So, I went for it, because I knew I could pay it off when both houses sold and…."

"Wait a minute. Wasn't that the year the housing market crashed?"

"Yep, I was right in the middle of buying and renovating foreclosed houses with tons of other investors. Fortunately for us, banks were handing out loans easily to families buying their first homes. The first house finally closed, but they postponed the closing on the second house several times in August and into September."

"Oh no, talk about stress!"

"Believe me, I was so nervous. OK, but here's the best part. We closed on the second house on the Friday in September, just before everything crashed the next week."

"No way! I can't believe how lucky you are! Talk about timing."

"Brenda, you're right. I was so lucky! The following year, Sam dangled another house for me to invest in and renovate, but I declined because I had enough stressful excitement."

—— *Mid-October 2018* ——

"Hey!"

"Hi, Brenda, I'm calling to check on you because when I visited you last month, you seemed like you were still getting over the Steve fiasco. How are you doing?"

"Not very well. I'm trying to figure out how I just didn't catch on to what Steve was all about. When we were dating, he took me to Vegas on business and we stayed at the penthouse of this incredible hotel. We could have just rented a room there… but the penthouse? Oh yeah, and my wedding ring cost beaucoup bucks. The reason I know is because we shopped for it together. He wanted it to be very special."

"One more thing added to his credit card debt, right?"

"Yeah, and he had already bought me a Promise Ring that had an amethyst surrounded by diamonds."

"That was a beautiful ring. Do you still have it?"

"Funny you should ask. About a month after the

*annulment, he asked very politely in his manner, that
if I didn't want it anymore, his daughter might like
to have it."*

"Really?"

*"I did send it to him. There really wasn't any reason for
me to keep it."*

"I guess you're right."

*"You know, my attorney asked me before the annulment
if I ever thought Steve married me for my money. It
seemed like an insult at the time. I just wasn't ready to
go there. I mean, he was always so loving and kind and
made me feel like my happiness was his top priority."*

"Brenda, it's understandable you're still grieving and
feeling confused and trying to make sense of it all.
I can imagine having his office furniture and clothes
still there to remind you, doesn't help."

*"Yeah, and he keeps sending me emails saying he's having
a hard time, living out of his car for a while and then on
his daughter's couch. He was disappointed we couldn't
work it out. I don't know what to do with his stuff. I just*

don't have the energy to deal with it. There's a lot of his kitchen pots and pans, special cooking utensils, spices, oils, and sauces. You name it, he had to have it all, because he loved to cook. In fact, when he moved out of his house to move in here, he sold most of his furniture, and brought his kitchen items to my house. Now I remember what he did. He rented a room for me and Chester at a very nice hotel catering to people with pets. He wanted me gone while he moved all his kitchen items into my house."

"Why did he want you gone?"

"I don't know. Maybe he thought it would be easier without my interfering. Of course, I wouldn't have, because I love being cooked for. That's just the way Steve was, always thinking of my comfort first."

———— *End of November 2018* ————

"Hey, Laura, how are you?"

"Great! Just checking on how your Thanksgiving went?"

"You know I'm so blessed with my two daughters and their children living nearby. My son and his new wife came so we could all be together for Thanksgiving. My daughter-in-law cooked the turkey, and the girls brought the fixings. How was yours?"

"I celebrated with my daughter, her husband and his family, and my grandchildren in October for their Canadian Thanksgiving. It was wonderful being with everyone. As for the November Thanksgiving here in Montana, a friend invited me to celebrate with her family and a few friends. It was fabulous!"

"Aren't you lucky to celebrate Thanksgiving twice?"

"Yeah, and I always look forward to turkey dinners because they're my favorite."

"I totally agree, and it's even better when someone else does the cooking. It's a big ordeal."

"Brenda, so how are you really doing? Did Steve ever get his office furniture and stuff?"

"No, but my son and his wife could see I didn't know what to do about it, and they offered a fabulous suggestion. In fact, they took care of contacting a moving company to drop off a storage pod. It amazed me that we filled it up. Oh, I meant to tell you that when I was packing up Steve's files and office supplies, there was no evidence of his $700,000 retirement fund or letters from any attorney or investment company. Don't you think that's kind of strange?"

"Definitely! And yet he kept all the credit cards and the letter from the debt relief company."

"Yeah, go figure."

"Anyway, it must have felt good to get his stuff out of your house."

"It sure did! Having his personal items here just kept reminding me of him and the life we had together."

"Is he going to pay for it?"

"Ah huh! I emailed him to say he'd have to pay for the pod storage and moving. He whined about having to pay for it. I don't know what he expected me to do with his stuff. Maybe he was hoping I'd change my mind and invite him back. I mean, with all the emails he keeps sending me, hoping we could work things out and saying I was the love of his life."

"Oh, Brenda, it's a shame Steve keeps sending those emails like he wants you to feel guilty or breakdown and invite him back."

"I just don't respond."

—— *Mid-January 2019* ——

"Hello, Brenda, funny you should call because I was thinking about you. How are you doing?"

"Hey, Laura, I'm doing okay, thank you very much. How was Christmas? Were you able to get to Canada for the Holidays?"

"Yes, just barely. I drove to my daughter's a few days earlier than I planned because there was another huge snowstorm coming. It was a wonderful Christmas with the grandkids and my daughter's husband's family. How about you?"

"It was very busy and fun shopping for the four grandchildren. Getting together with family makes it so special, right? Oh, and watching the little ones opening presents on Christmas morning. That's the best part!"

"Speaking of family, did you happen to see your ex at any of the events?"

"Now that I have two exes, and yes, I know who you're talking about. He just ignores me, which is so much better

than getting angry looks all the time. I'm sure his change in attitude is because he doesn't have to send me alimony checks anymore."

"I was talking to Sam the other day, and he mentioned you're thinking about selling your house."

"Well, I have to do something because I'm struggling financially. I may have to, because I'm not getting the income as I did before Steve. Sam suggested I turn the one-bedroom apartment in my basement into an Airbnb, which he says would bring more income than renting it out long term."

"Sounds like a great idea! Sam is awesome and goes beyond just being a real estate agent. I can imagine it would be difficult to give up your beautiful home. It's in a perfect location, next to hiking trails into the mountains and close to town. You probably won't have any trouble renting the little apartment as an Airbnb."

———— *End of February 2019* ————

"Hey, Laura, how are you today?"

"Great! You know, next time we talk, let's use FaceTime."

*"Well, I'm glad we aren't using it today because I have a
gloomy face on. I know it sounds silly, but I'm not in the
greatest mood this morning. Somehow getting up and
seeing it still snowing on top of tons of snow, meaning
I can't even get out to walk Chester. But otherwise,
I'll get myself back up."*

"I know you will. But look what you're still dealing
with? Not only are you grieving the loss of a relationship
and the financial stress is scary at our age."

*"No argument there. What perpetuates this feeling of
confusion and guilt and anger at myself for not recogniz-
ing the red flags from the beginning is Steve sending me
a Birthday email. He attached a YouTube link to a video
wishing me love and happiness."*

"He did? I'm surprised that he's still trying to stay
connected."

"And then he just sent me a Happy Valentine's present of expensive chocolates. What is he thinking? If only he would stop fooling himself. I wanted to write him a very long letter and list everything he did to me in the order it happened. But I don't think that would help anything, just make me feel better for a short time. I've actually written this letter and destroyed it and then wrote it again, then destroyed it."

"I think I'd question his motives for continuing to remind you of his love. Is he wanting forgiveness or to punish you in a sick way?"

"It's the same feeling of grief from a death because it's about loss. I think this kind of grief is even more difficult because they're still out there. You have this tremendous loss and hurt and pain and betrayal, and they're still out there. I spoke with my sister-in-law when her husband died of colon cancer. She can grieve him being gone. Even though it's very painful, there is a finality about it. Believe me, I know grief from losing members of my family. But a painful divorce or annulment and having that person around just seems more difficult. Steve is in California but still walking around, living in his new apartment, continuing to lead his life. My niece told me she saw him in a bar at a fancy hotel near her. She was shocked to see

him there. She recognized him and took a photo and text it to me. That devastated me! I think it's easier to visit a grave."

——— March 2019 ———

"Hey!"

"Hi, Brenda. How are you doing? Did you get rid of your gloomy face since the last time we talked?"

"Very funny! I'm doing much better. The sun is out, and Chester and I were walking through the neighborhood and we're just walking in the front door."

"Do you want me to call you back?"

"No, are you kidding? I enjoy talking to you and now that I have you, how are you?"

"Well, I have a story that might make you feel better to know that you're not alone in meeting men that misrepresent themselves."

"OK, you've got my attention."

"Do you remember my telling you about a guy I dated last year, Dwight? I met him on Match."

"Right. I remember him. He sounded like a nice guy."

"He grew up on a horse ranch, very mannerly and respectful. We went to a horse jumping event, watched the sunset at a tiki bar on the lake, and hiked in the nearby mountains. Whenever he invited me out for dinner or a movie, he always paid."

"He sounds like fun. How long did you date him?"

"During the four months that we dated, he told me he was retired and was my age. We exchanged stories about our careers and where we lived… meaning city and states. There were a couple of things that made me feel uncomfortable. When we met for dinner or at a bar, he was a little too loud for me. He was one of those guys who had to be the center of attention."

"Could be a red flag waving at you, right?"

"Yep, and in our getting to know each other, he wasn't forthcoming with personal information. Most of the time, people like to talk about themselves, but with him it was like pulling teeth. The fact that he was evasive about personal information made me question who he really was. I decided to look him up on the state website for convicted felons."

"For real, Laura? You never told me about your suspicions."

"I'll tell you why in a minute. I searched his name on this website and his photo came right up. It said he was on parole for embezzlement and his parole would expire in the next month."

"Wow! It's amazing the information we can get on the internet. Did it give any details about the embezzlement charge?"

"No, no more info. But I'll tell you, it scared the daylights out of me! The reason I didn't tell anyone is that I was embarrassed for being so trusting. You wonder who he stole from. You know, it could have been from the company he previously worked for or maybe an unsuspecting female. She could have fallen in love with him and lost a lot of money. Maybe she pressed charges. Who knows?"

"Oh, Laura, I am so sorry. I can relate to that. I felt ashamed that I believed him and too embarrassed to discuss it with anyone. It took two years before I told you about all the details."

"Believe me, since I had that experience, I can empathize with you for those emotions. There was no loss when I ended that relationship."

"Did you tell him what you found out?"

"No, I didn't feel comfortable to put him on the spot. We hadn't known each other long enough for a love relationship to develop. We had a disagreement about something, so I let that be my excuse for ending it."

———— *Fast Forward to April 2020* ————

"Hi, Brenda!"

"Hey, Laura, how ya doin'?"

"Well, it's great to be back home safely in Montana!"

"I was so looking forward to visiting you in Florida, but the coronavirus hit. You mentioned that you had trouble getting a flight home."

"It was a crazy time trying to get a flight out of Tampa. They closed the beaches March 20th, cancelled all hotel reservations, and sent people home. It looked like a ghost town with hotel parking lots empty, museums and galleries closed, restaurants and coffee shops only serving takeout. I felt really bad for the business owners. All of us tourists were scrambling to get reservations at the end of March. Then mine was cancelled but rescheduled for the next day. Good thing I hadn't checked out of my condo yet."

"Wow, I had no idea. Are you staying safe and healthy?"

"Oh yes! And how are you doing? I'm asking because you said Steve was still sending you gifts."

"Yeah, can you believe it? He sends an email or a gift every four to six months. I mean, it's been two years since the annulment!"

"Sounds like he doesn't want you to forget him. I just don't understand what's up with him. Do you?"

"No, I don't get it. But I have to tell you about his most recent emails, which are upsetting. His first email was commenting on the increase in COVID in my county and he asked how I was and if my family was okay. I did write a short response saying we were all fine, and I hoped his family was fine too. Then he sends a newsy email about his son and daughter and that he's been going back and forth for business."

"Wait, you're saying he's been in your area? Seems kind of unusual as I remember most of his consulting jobs were out of state."

"He said his consulting business was picking up. I shouldn't have answered his first email because he went on to say he couldn't understand why we weren't together. And this is where it gets disturbing. He tried to give

excuses for why he had to borrow money from me, and that he had very little debt when we met. He felt most of the debt was created by us!!!"

"No!"

"Also, he said he never should have sold his house and it could have been handled differently. He made it sound like I was just as responsible for the spending, like I was demanding to continue our expensive lifestyle."

"Oh no! I think he's becoming delusional. With all his debts, how could he possibly pay you back without selling his house? It sounds like he wants you to assume some responsibility for his taking your money."

"Right! And get this. He still claims his friend stole his retirement fund. You know, after I discovered the truth about the fictitious attorney and investment company in Houston, I never challenged him on the truth."

"Good for you. I don't think it would've gotten you anywhere. What do you think?"

"The reason I didn't challenge him on it is because I just didn't want to hear any more lies. It's still so painful to think about it."

"Do you regret the decisions you made?"

"Not for a minute. I believe I did what I had to do to survive. Just the same, it still hurts to get his emails. Oh, and here is the last sentence in his email where he twists the knife, 'We were meant to be together and maybe we could forget the past.' I just felt like screaming!"

"No way! I'm right there screaming with you! Why don't you block his emails?"

"Well, as long as he keeps sending the $200 a month to pay off what he owes me, I feel like I should keep the communication open. I do know that I will not respond to any more of his emails. It's like he's sticking the knife in and saying he loves me at the same time. That's just sick, don't you think?"

"Totally! I hope he doesn't try to see you when he's in the area. Do you think he would do that?"

"Hard to say."

PART IV
Resources

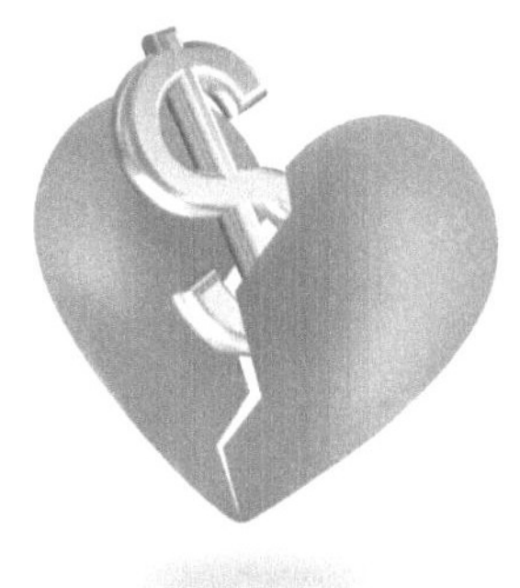

A Note from the Author

If this is the first time you've heard about financial infidelity, you're not alone. According to the latest research, financial infidelity is on the rise. Trent Hamm, founder of *The Simple Dollar* explains that "When one spouse is making significant financial moves without the knowledge of the other, it endangers the financial future of both people…" Typical examples involve hiding credit cards, compulsive shopping, lying about net worth or career/occupation, gambling debts, secret loans, draining savings and retirement accounts.

Let's be perfectly clear. Financial infidelity has the potential to be as harmful to a healthy relationship as sexual infidelity. When the deception is exposed, feelings of betrayal and growing distrust weakens the foundation of commitment. Can this be a disease of chronic lying? Will therapy help and is there hope for the relationship? My curiosity to learn more about the prevention and healing from financial infidelity, compelled me to form a list of books and websites to share with you. However, you will notice the list of resources is short.

I'm very grateful to Brenda for letting me share her story. In fact, she hopes this will open the eyes of unsuspecting women, especially in retirement. For those entering a new relationship that may become a committed one, her advice is to pay attention to the red flags, ask questions and plan an Experian Party to check each other's credit ratings. If there are differences in spending habits or financial planning, hopefully, an honest discussion will lead to an agreeable strategy. If the relationship is worth pursuing, consider financial therapy.

Financial Infidelity Resources

Suggested Books:

The Heart of Money: A Couple's Guide to Creating True Financial Intimacy by Deborah L. Price. You will learn strategies and tools for creating financial intimacy while learning to communicate about money issues calmly rather than reactively.

Mind over Money: Overcoming the Money Disorders That Threaten Our Financial Health by Bradley Klontz and Ted Klontz. This father and son team describe the 12 most common "money disorders," and explain how to identify them. This book will teach you how to have that financial conversation and help repair a dysfunctional relationship with money.

Financial Infidelity: Seven Steps to Conquering the #1 Relationship Wrecker by Bonnie Eaker Weil, PhD. The author is an internationally acclaimed relationship therapist, offering 30 years of counseling on the relationship of intimacy and money.

Smart Women Finish Rich: Expanded and Updated by David Bach. He is a *New York Times* Bestselling author of several books. He not only empowers women but people of all ages.

Rewire for Wealth: Three Steps Any Woman Can Take to Program Her Brain for Financial Success by Barbara Huson who is a financial therapist and understands first hand financial infidelity. Barbara offers a unique approach combining mind, body, spirit and the power of the brain.

Your Credit Score: How to Improve the 3-Digit Number That Shapes your Financial Future by Liz Weston. Her book is an up-to-date guide to new laws and rules with crucial information for protecting or rebuilding your credit score.

Suggested Websites:

www.nfcc.org
National Foundation for Credit Counseling. This nonprofit organization helps people overcome their money issues and offers financial education and counseling services.

www.thesimpledollar.com/financial-wellness
Google the articles, "Ten Red Flags of Financial Infidelity" and "What to Do About it," by Trent Hamm.

www.financialtherapyassociation.org
Financial Therapy Association offers articles, research and a list of Financial Therapists by State.

www.moneycoachinginstitute.com
Locate a Certified Money Coach to help clients solve common problems associated with money choices, unconscious patterns, and beliefs that restrict them from reaching their full financial potential.

www.nefe.org
National Endowment for Financial Education is an independent, centralizing voice providing leadership, research and collaboration to advance financial well-being.

About the Author

Laura L. Whittemore has been a life coach for sixteen years. She coauthored two books with Mary Ann Keatley, PhD, CCC, *Recovering from Mild Traumatic Brain Injury (MTBI): A Handbook of Hope for Our Military Warriors and Their Families*, as well as, *Understanding Mild Traumatic Brain Injury (MTBI): An Insightful Guide to Symptoms, Treatments and Redefining Recovery*. Laura has two children and six grandchildren and lives, writes, hikes and dances in northwest Montana.

Discussion Questions

Why do you think Brenda decided to accept the marriage proposal from Steve?

What elements of their relationship allowed Steve to influence Brenda?

Why did Brenda wait two years before sharing her suspicions with her close friend, Laura, or other friends?

If you were Brenda, what would you have done differently?

If Steve tried to connect with Brenda five years later, do you think she would agree to meet with him?

Would you consider Steve a giver or a taker? Why?

Does this story remind you of someone in a similar situation?

Does this story cause you to question your knowledge of the financial situation in your marriage or partnership? Even if you've been married for over 20 years?

YOUR RECOMMENDATION
IS SO VALUABLE!

If you enjoyed this book, please tell a friend or your Book Club. Also, I would so appreciate your leaving a review even if it's a sentence or two.